# Developing Cultural Adaptability

## How to Work Across Differences

IDEAS INTO ACTION GUIDEBOOKS

Aimed at managers and executives who are concerned with their own and
others' development, each guidebook in this series gives specific advice on
how to complete a developmental task or solve a leadership problem.

| | |
|---|---|
| LEAD CONTRIBUTORS | Jennifer J. Deal |
| | Don W. Prince |
| CONTRIBUTORS | Maxine Dalton |
| | Michael Hoppe |
| | Meena Wilson |
| GUIDEBOOK ADVISORY GROUP | Victoria A. Guthrie |
| | Cynthia D. McCauley |
| | Ellen Van Velsor |
| | |
| DIRECTOR OF PUBLICATIONS | Martin Wilcox |
| EDITOR | Peter Scisco |
| DESIGN AND LAYOUT | Joanne Ferguson |
| CONTRIBUTING ARTISTS | Laura J. Gibson |
| | Chris Wilson, 29 & Company |

CCL No. 422
ISBN No. 1-882197-80-1

CENTER FOR CREATIVE LEADERSHIP
POST OFFICE BOX 26300
GREENSBORO, NORTH CAROLINA 27438-6300
336-288-7210
WWW.CCL.ORG / PUBLICATIONS

AN IDEAS INTO ACTION GUIDEBOOK

# Developing Cultural Adaptability

## How to Work Across Differences

Jennifer J. Deal and Don W. Prince

Center for ®
**Creative Leadership**
leadership. learning. life.

This series of guidebooks draws on the practical knowledge that the Center for Creative Leadership (CCL®) has generated in the course of more than thirty years of research and educational activity conducted in partnership with hundreds of thousands of managers and executives. Much of this knowledge is shared – in a way that is distinct from the typical university department, professional association, or consultancy. CCL is not simply a collection of individual experts, although the individual credentials of its staff are impressive; rather it is a community, with its members holding certain principles in common and working together to understand and generate practical responses to today's leadership and organizational challenges.

The purpose of the series is to provide managers with specific advice on how to complete a developmental task or solve a leadership challenge. In doing that, the series carries out CCL's mission to advance the understanding, practice, and development of leadership for the benefit of society worldwide. We think you will find the Ideas Into Action Guidebooks an important addition to your leadership toolkit.

# Table of Contents

## EXECUTIVE BRIEF

Thinking about cultural differences around the world isn't just an intellectual exercise for managers working in an increasingly global environment. Being able to communicate effectively across cultural differences, understanding how to negotiate complex social situations, and being familiar with the customs and norms of many cultures are important skills in organizations today. Perhaps even more important than possessing those essential pieces of cultural knowledge is the skill of *cultural adaptability* – the willingness and ability to recognize, understand, and work effectively across cultural differences. Proficiency in cultural adaptability helps contemporary managers to build the relationships needed to achieve results in today's global organizations, especially when those relationships are forged across borders and cultures. It enables them to interact effectively with people different from themselves, whether these people work on the next floor or on the other side of the world.

# What Is Cultural Adaptability?

Today's global workplace is more diverse and complex than ever before. When organizations have business units, customers, and employees scattered around the world, managers find they must work across time, distance, and cultures. To build and maintain relationships that allow them to work effectively with others in such circumstances, managers have to figure out what the differences and similarities are between them and others with whom they work. Those differences affect expectations, approaches to work, views of authority, and other issues. They make managerial work more complex, and call for a new kind of flexibility for handling differences and change – *cultural adaptability*.

Cultural adaptability is the willingness and ability to recognize, understand, and work effectively across cultures. It presumes that such interactions will have successful outcomes (tasks are completed, goals are met, and the people involved are satisfied with their professional relationships). The implication for managers who want to be or remain successful is clear. Cultural adaptability is an essential competency for leading in a global environment.

# Why Is Cultural Adaptability Important?

Employees at all levels of contemporary organizations bring different values, expectations, and perspectives – their culture – with them to work. Those differences affect how individuals in these organizations lead, manage, and interact with others, and how the work gets done.

There are many definitions of culture, but one common idea explicit in all of the definitions is that culture is shared. Culture includes, among other things, beliefs about what is acceptable or unacceptable conduct within a society or group of people. It includes deeply held values and beliefs that influence behavior which can be interpreted in many different ways by people outside of that

## When Worlds Collide

For a dramatic view of how cultural differences affect results, consider the example of the $125 million Mars Climate Orbiter. The National Aeronautics and Space Administration launched that spacecraft at the end of 1998 for a mission that would put it in orbit around the red planet about a year later. Two teams of engineers working on the orbiter's navigational software carried out their work using two incompatible measuring systems – metric (meters and grams, for example) and English (feet and pounds, for example). The project's leadership did not notice, or did not check, whether the unit translations had been carried out. Each team assumed that its method was correct and did not expect that the other team would use a different method. On September 23, 1999, the orbiter approached Mars at an altitude of about 37 miles, instead of the planned 93 miles. Plunging into the planet's thin atmosphere, it incinerated within minutes.

Why did each team believe its method was correct? Because each was working under a particular set of rules, norms, and expectations. People often assume that others act under the same set of rules as they do. When they don't meet those expectations, conflict (and even disaster) results.

culture. Culture also includes expectations about how people will behave in particular situations or relationships.

Many employees today – many people generally – understand that they work with, serve, and are surrounded by people with different mind-sets and expectations based on different backgrounds. Many employees, although not all, may also understand that responding to those people with "that isn't the way we do things here" just isn't going to work in a world that grows ever more connected. Managers often interact daily with peers, bosses, direct reports, and others from different cultures, and they often handle those interactions poorly, causing avoidable misunderstandings, frustrations, and stress.

As a manager you can't expect to know exactly how to behave in every different place or with every different person. But you can appreciate the importance of a skill such as cultural adaptability, because the people with whom you work think and act differently from you. If you want an example, start with yourself. The worksheet on pages 10–11 can help you understand how developed your cultural adaptability is.

After completing the cultural adaptability worksheet, you should have a good idea of your ability to work with others who are culturally different from you. Regardless of your score, you'll benefit from developing your cultural adaptability throughout your career because it will enhance your effectiveness and flexibility as a manager.

# Cultural Adaptability Worksheet

This short activity deals with attitudes and behaviors that are important for working with people from other countries. Rate your present level of skill on a scale of 0 to 5 as described below, and write the corresponding number in the blank to the right of each statement. This worksheet is for your use only, so be as candid as possible. The scale is

5 = one of my greatest strengths
4 = something I am good at
3 = something I can do but I need to improve a little
2 = something I can do but I need to improve a lot
1 = something I am not able to do
0 = don't know

I can operate effectively in a foreign language, even if through translation. _____

I am sensitive to differences between cultures. _____

I work hard to understand the perspectives of people from other cultures when we are working together. _____

I like to experience different cultures. _____

I am quick to change my behavior to match a new environment (for example, when assigned to a foreign country). _____

I enjoy the challenge of working in countries other than my own. _____

I understand how culture influences the way people express disagreement. _____

I can use cultural differences as a source of strength for the organization. _____

I am aware of my own deeply held beliefs when dealing with others. _____

I know when to hold fast to personal values and when to consider others' values. _____

I effectively surface my own and others' deeply held assumptions, values, or beliefs before making important decisions. _____

I can manage culture shock. _____

I can adapt my management style to meet cultural expectations. _____

*Total score*_____

## Worksheet Scoring

| | | |
|---|---|---|
| 32–42 (lowest 25%) | Novice | I have limited experience working across cultures and am not particularly aware of the ways this influences my interactions. |
| 43–52 (middle 50%) | Intermediate | With conscious effort, I can anticipate cultural differences, see others' perspectives, and change the way I interact with them. |
| 53–64 (highest 25%) | Expert | I am able to easily work across cultures, perhaps in multiple languages. I am knowledgeable about many cultures, and can adopt an appropriate style for most interactions. |

# Developing Your Cultural Adaptability

Your cultural adaptability will increase as you gain knowledge and skills that you can use to interact effectively with people different from yourself. What does it take to develop cultural adaptability? Four components are necessary.

- **Examine** your cultural foundations.
- **Expect** to encounter cultural differences.
- **Educate** yourself about different cultures.
- **Experience** cross-cultural interactions and learn from them.

## Examine Your Cultural Foundations

Developing cultural adaptability doesn't mean changing who you are or giving up your cultural identity. (Even if you work in another country or culture you might learn to adapt, but your basic cultural orientation is unlikely to change.) One component of developing cultural adaptability is understanding your own cultural background and how it affects you. Each of us operates in a "cultural comfort zone" and sees the world through the lens of a particular cultural conditioning. Culture influences our perceptions in a given situation, our interpretations of others' behaviors, and our actions and reactions. Awareness of these influences is necessary for developing cross-cultural flexibility.

Being more fully aware of our cultural foundations helps us avoid unconsciously judging others or expecting others to think, feel, and behave as we do. Prejudging is a natural reaction when these interactions push us out of our comfort zone. Most of us prefer what is predictable, familiar, and comfortable. When we are faced with difference, we may feel stimulated and move to embrace it. But as we move farther and farther away from our comfort zone (especially if we are dealing with differences that threaten our ways of explaining the world), there is a tendency for us to retreat to where we feel more comfortable in what CCL calls the "jump-back response."

Jumping back isn't wrong. It's actually necessary for us to retreat from a new experience so we can reflect on it, understand it, and integrate it into our understanding of the world. One way to increase your cultural adaptability is to stretch yourself beyond your comfort zone and stay longer in areas that are unfamiliar and uncomfortable. True, it's uncomfortable to increase your exposure to different people and their way of doing things. To make the best use of your natural jump-back response, try to stay longer in the "uncomfortable" place while making sure you have the chance to retreat to where you are comfortable. That respite gives you the time and space to integrate new experiences into your stock of cultural intelligence and to gain the confidence to venture out again.

## Expect to Encounter Cultural Differences

Effective managers are alert to the impact of cultural differences in the workplace. They look for clues that these differences might be at work in a certain interaction. Clues include such things as confusion, frustration, anxiety, irritation, and miscommunication. These are often present when cultural differences are at play.

Although it's possible to overemphasize cultural differences, the greater danger for managers is their minimizing the differences, only to be caught off guard when conflict, performance problems, or other leadership challenges arise. This is particularly true in relationships where the differences may be subtle or beneath the surface. Consider two members of a global team, for example, who come from Australia and the United States. Because of certain external similarities (skin color and common language, to name two), they unconsciously assume that they view the world alike. But they are surprised and confused when their different attitudes concerning authority, personal achievement, and humor cause mild frustration and misunderstanding. Those feelings and reactions may hinder the work of the team – the work for which you, as their manager, are responsible. Identifying differences that can cause confusion or conflict is a good step toward developing more flexibility in your relationships with people who are different from yourself – in other words, building cultural adaptability.

## Educate Yourself about Different Cultures

One way to increase your understanding of cultural differences so that you can more quickly spot clues that point to differences is to learn more about how various cultures view important aspects of work and life. Seven broad cultural dimensions in particular are useful in explaining those differences.

1. source and expressions of identity (collective/individual)
2. source and expressions of authority (equal/unequal)
3. goals and means of achievement (tough/tender)
4. response to uncertainty and change (dynamic/stable)
5. means of knowledge acquisition (active/reflective)
6. orientation to time (scarce/plentiful)
7. response to natural and social environment (doing/being)

Although some part of all of these seven dimensions is present in each culture, different cultures place more or less importance on each one. These dimensions are especially noticeable when comparing cultures of different countries. Review the descriptions on pages 15-21 to see how different cultures line up in their views of work and life.

Cultural Dimension 1
## Source and Expressions of Identity

*Collective* ⊕ ⊕ ⊕ ⊕ ⊕ ⊕ ⊕ ⊕ ⊕ ⊕ ⊕ ⊕ *Individual*

| | |
|---|---|
| People in cultures near the *collective* end of the continuum define themselves more in terms of the organization, tribe, clan, or extended family to which they belong. They expect, and are expected, to show loyalty and support toward their group or organization in return for protection, lifetime employment, and a sense of belonging. Countries where you might expect to encounter this view include Mexico, China, and Indonesia. | People in cultures near the *individual* end of the continuum define themselves primarily through their own achievements and their immediate family. They expect, and are expected, to be self-reliant, show initiative, and chart their own career. Countries where you might expect to encounter this view include the United States, Australia, and Sweden. |

Do you have difficulty with people expecting unreasonable levels of loyalty? Do you have difficulty with people not being as loyal as they should be? How do these cultural differences affect your work? How do you react to these differences? How might you change your reactions and behavior to account for and to accommodate these cultural differences in values and perspectives?

Cultural Dimension 2
## Source and Expressions of Authority

*Equal* 🌐 🌐 🌐 🌐 🌐 🌐 🌐 🌐 🌐 🌐 🌐 🌐 🌐 *Unequal*

People in cultures near the *equal* end of the scale expect that differences in power among members of that culture will be minimized. They look on hierarchical structures as an expression of inequality in roles, established for convenience or efficiency, not as a description of their value to the society. They want "superiors" to be accessible and to consult with them. Those with and without power alike see themselves as existentially equal. Countries where you might expect to encounter this view include Denmark, Sweden, and the United States.

People in cultures near the *unequal* end of the scale expect and accept large differences in power, status, and privileges. Hierarchies are considered an expression of this inequality and satisfy a need for dependence, structure, and security. They prefer superiors to be benevolent autocrats who take the initiative, make the decisions, and take care of their subordinates' needs. Those with power and those without do not see themselves as existentially equal. Countries where you might expect to encounter this view include Saudi Arabia, Mexico, and the Philippines.

Do you have difficulty with people who expect to be treated exactly like the person in charge? Do you have difficulty with people who refuse to treat their direct reports with adequate respect because they are at a lower level in the organization? How do these cultural differences affect your work? How do you react to these differences? How might you change your reactions and behavior to account for and to accommodate these cultural differences in values and perspectives?

## Cultural Dimension 3
## Goals and Means of Achievement

*Tough*            *Tender*

People from cultures near the *tough* end of the scale strive for tangible signs of success and progress, such as high income, career advancement, or working for a prestigious company. They want to excel and have great admiration for achievers. Work plays a central role in their lives. They value competition and decisiveness. Countries where you might expect to encounter this view include Japan, Mexico, and the United States.

People from cultures near the *tender* end of the scale strive for cooperation, consensus, and solidarity among members of their own and others' society. They have empathy for the less fortunate and value modesty. They prefer the slogan "work to live" over "live to work." They place greater value on intangible achievements, such as good work relationships, time for family and friends, or serving others. Countries where you might expect to encounter this view include Denmark, Norway, and Sweden.

Do you have difficulty with people who put relationships ahead of getting results? Do you have difficulty with people who are willing to step on others to get results? How do these cultural differences affect your work? How do you react to these differences? How might you change your reactions and behavior to account for and to accommodate these cultural differences in values and perspectives?

## Cultural Dimension 4
## Response to Uncertainty and Change

*Dynamic* ⊕ ⊕ ⊕ ⊕ ⊕ ⊕ ⊕ ⊕ ⊕ ⊕ ⊕ ⊕ ⊕ *Stable*

In cultures near the *dynamic* end of the scale, people accept uncertainty or ambiguity as a natural part of life. They accept conflict, dissent, and competition as normal; in fact, they view them as potentially beneficial. They are willing to take risks even in unfamiliar circumstances. They value flexibility and adaptability, and are open to adjusting existing rules or regulations as the situation dictates. Countries where you might expect to encounter this view include Denmark, Sweden, and the United States.

In cultures near the *stable* end of the scale, people are more likely to shun unfamiliar risks or unpredictable situations. They get nervous when encountering changes, conflict, or competition in their work and will try to avoid them using clearly defined rules, regulations, and policies. Uncertainty causes significant discomfort and stress, and they feel compelled to avoid mistakes and failure. Countries where you might expect to encounter this view include Greece, France, and Japan.

Do you have difficulty with people who want to change things all the time for no apparent reason? Do you have difficulty with people who resist every change that comes along? How do these cultural differences affect your work? How do you react to these differences? How might you change your reactions and behavior to account for and to accommodate these cultural differences in values and perspectives?

Cultural Dimension 5
## Means of Knowledge Acquisition

*Active*          *Reflective*

People from cultures at the *active* end of the scale value facts, empirical data, and practical experience. They are willing to experiment and solve problems by trial and error. Case studies, experiential learning, and fieldwork appeal to them. They value the scientific method (observe, hypothesize, test) of identifying and solving problems. Countries where you might expect to encounter this view include the United States, Sweden, and the Netherlands.

People from cultures at the *reflective* end of the scale value conceptual models to guide their actions. They prefer to understand the general principles behind the problem or to develop an intuitive feel for it before attempting a solution. They admire intellectual brilliance and deductive reasoning, but feel little need to experiment to achieve a solution. They value great thinkers over doers. Countries where you might expect to encounter this view include France, Mexico, and Saudi Arabia.

Do you have difficulty with people who try things without first thinking much about them? Do you have difficulty with people who prefer spending extensive periods of time thinking about and analyzing a problem (paralysis by analysis, some people call it)? How do these cultural differences affect your work? How do you react to these differences? How might you change your reactions and behavior to account for and to accommodate these cultural differences in values and perspectives?

## Cultural Dimension 6
## Orientation to Time

*Scarce* 🌍 🌍 🌍 🌍 🌍 🌍 🌍 🌍 🌍 🌍 🌍 🌍 🌍 *Plentiful*

People from cultures near the *scarce* side of the scale treat time as a limited resource. They see time as linear and life as sequential, working in the present toward the future. They believe that time ought not to be wasted. They want meetings to start on time, they like to stay busy, and they need to see results in the short term. They believe that every minute should be used wisely, and they place a value on their own and others' time. Countries where you might expect to encounter this view include the United States, Germany, and Australia.

People from countries near the *plentiful* end of the scale treat time as infinitely available. In their view time cannot be wasted. Timeliness or deadlines are seen as expressions of intent, not as commitments. They prefer a life that evolves from the moment and allows for multiple and simultaneous involvement with the people and opportunities around them. They honor the past to fully live in the present, and do not see value in achieving deadlines or doing things on time. Countries where you might expect to encounter this view include Mexico, Iran, and Saudi Arabia.

Do you have difficulty with people who do not respect your time? Do you have difficulty with people being too rigid about schedules and deadlines? How do these cultural differences affect your work? How do you react to these differences? How might you change your reactions and behavior to account for and to accommodate these cultural differences in values and perspectives?

Cultural Dimension 7
## Response to Natural and Social Environment

*Doing*            *Being*

People from cultures at the *doing* end of the scale prefer to proactively shape their lives and surroundings. They value planned activities that improve their conditions. Technology is used as a means of making progress toward a better or more fulfilled life. Being in control over one's life and environment is valued. Countries where you might expect to encounter this view include China, Japan, and the United States.

People from cultures at the *being* end of the scale feel a need to live within the natural limits of their environment. They see themselves as a part of their environment and accept what life gives them. They do not seek to change or control their environment through the use of technology. They prefer a steady and relaxed way of life that allows them to live in the here and now. They trust that "things will work out"; harmony with the world around them is valued. Countries where you might expect to encounter this view include France, Sweden, and Norway.

Do you have difficulty with people who need to control their surroundings? Do you have difficulty with people who are unwilling to take control of their environment? How do these cultural differences affect your work? How do you react to these differences? How might you change your reactions and behavior to account for and to accommodate these cultural differences in values and perspectives?

Compare the descriptions and examples in the cultural dimensions tables to your own experiences. Can you see differences between yourself and others that are related to these different cultural dimensions? Reviewing these descriptions of cultural dimensions is just one of many learning opportunities you can use to increase understanding of other cultures. Your capacity to learn about other cultures extends beyond books and foreign language courses, which are also important. It includes your experiences with other cultures and your ability to learn from those experiences. Here are some suggestions for activities that will provide you with a range of learning experiences and opportunities.

**Learn from others.** There may be individuals in your organization who have a high level of cultural awareness and experience. Seek them out as coaches or role models. Some may be true global leaders, able to manage across cultures, countries, and time zones. Others may be able to relate to anyone across differences. Learn what skills they possess and how they developed them. Another type of coach might be culture-specific – someone who can help you establish and nurture relationships with those from within his or her culture. Before traveling to work in India for the first time, for example, you might invite an Indian friend and colleague to lunch to answer questions, give advice, and confirm if what the guidebooks say is accurate.

**Look for on-the job challenges.** Cross-cultural challenges may already be present in your job or can be sought out as a developmental experience. Are your employees, team members, or customers culturally diverse? If so, you're already in one of the most effective learning laboratories available. Perhaps you have an opportunity to participate in or lead a geographically dispersed team or a global project. Are you open to an international assignment sometime in your career? Many managers report that these types of challenges are rewarding and effective at building cultural

adaptability. You don't have to start with an international assignment, however. You can also seek challenges in smaller spheres.
For example, you could volunteer to help host international managers from your organization when they visit your area.

**Travel internationally when you can.** Traveling to another
country either for business or personal reasons is a real possibility
for many people. If the opportunity arises, go beyond the chartered
tour approach to really experience the new culture. Don't limit
yourself to the standard tourist areas and attractions. To get a feel
for a new place, try visiting a bookstore, grocery market, café, and a
university student center. If you have a host from within that
country, the learning experience can be much richer.

**Experience different cultures where you are.** Most of us
don't have to get on a plane to experience a variety of cultures.
There are other ways to broaden our cultural horizons. Something
as simple as choosing a new restaurant or broadening your choice
of movies can be a cultural learning experience. Foreign films,
television, or videos open a window onto other cultures and are
full of historical and local references that carry specific cultural
messages. The film *Crouching Tiger, Hidden Dragon,* for example,
released in the United States in December 2000, provides insight
into Eastern mysticism and Buddhism, Chinese mythology, the role
of loyalty and honor in that culture, and the historical social taboos
that placed men and women in different roles.

Most cities support cultural events that showcase music,
drama, dance, and art from around the world. There are also ethnic
fairs, markets, and other venues that will give you a taste of other
cultures. Look for opportunities to engage in volunteer activities
that allow you to interact across cultures, such as teaching a language class, tutoring, working with refugees, and coaching
children's sports.

**Learn another language.** The more languages you speak, the more likely you are to score high on cultural adaptability. Speaking another language predisposes you to be more innovative, have greater business savvy, and adapt more readily to cultural differences in the workplace. In addition, every language you speak helps you understand at least one other culture because language and syntax reflect much of a culture's way of thinking. Learning any major language puts you in a position to relate more effectively to millions of other people. Even if you're not prepared to become fluent in several languages, you can enhance your cultural adaptability by learning basic greetings and vocabulary.

**Attend a leadership training or executive education course in another country.** Executive education courses provide a safe learning environment in which you can interact with peers from different countries, try new foods, learn others' perspectives on your home culture, and otherwise experience and learn from cultural differences. Adding a weekend excursion will enhance your cultural learning.

**Read about other cultures.** You can learn much about other cultures by reading some of the historical, geographical, and political information that's available. For example, reading a history of Spain helps you to understand why the Castilian city of Madrid is so different from Catalonian Barcelona (and why it may be important to know that when interacting with a Spaniard). Also, keeping current on news and world events is vitally important for a culturally literate person. The Internet and cable news channels make that daily task much easier. International papers like the *International Herald Tribune* and *The Economist* all appear on the Internet, and most news channels feature broadcasts from around the world. In addition to reading about other cultures, an effective learning tactic is to read the fictional literature of other cultures to see examples of cultural influence on common human themes.

**Practice people watching.** Watching others is a good way to learn more about how people behave, and can possibly give you a better understanding of your own reactions to their behavior. Observe a wide variety of people around you. You can learn about such things as personal space needs, beliefs about the use of public space, whether people linger over food, and what behaviors make you uncomfortable and might cause you to react negatively toward someone else. The more you learn about others and about yourself from this sort of experience, the more culturally adaptable you become because you will understand your own triggers and be able to alter your reactions.

What do these suggestions have in common? They force you to think and act beyond your cultural comfort zone. Engaging in these activities doesn't guarantee cultural adaptability, but the more of these tactics you choose to use, the greater the probability that you will develop new ways of thinking and acting.

## Experience Cross-cultural Interactions and Learn from Them

Have you ever been in a situation where something funny, embarrassing, or strange happened because of a cultural misunderstanding? For example, have you ever ordered the wrong meal because you didn't understand the menu, or used unacceptable slang because you didn't understand the nuances of a foreign language? Almost everyone can recall similar situations. These personal stories are rich learning opportunities because the cultural differences are so obvious that you clearly remember your reaction (maybe you laughed at your mistake, or maybe you were embarrassed and rushed to apologize).

Think back to a situation you experienced when something disconcerting or confusing happened because of a cultural misunderstanding. After you have thought through the entire incident, analyze it using the following questions: Why was it disconcerting/

confusing? What was misunderstood? Why was it misunderstood? What (specifically) were the different perspectives in play during the incident? What did you learn from the incident? How has what you learned from this affected what you do now? If you didn't learn anything, or if your behavior has not changed at all, why not?

Analyzing and reflecting on these experiences can help you understand your response when cultural differences make you feel uncomfortable – a fourth component of developing cultural adaptability. Use what you learned from these experiences to figure out what differences caused your response. If necessary, change your behavior so that you act in ways that alleviate conflict, create trust, and promote personal and organizational effectiveness.

This analysis of your experiences and responses puts you in the role of what might be called a *roving anthropologist*. In this role you observe, form hypotheses, test your ideas, and continually refine what you learn. Use the information you glean from this process to understand the situation, to understand the cultural perspectives of the other people who are part of the interaction, and to decide how to act effectively in the situation. It's not an easy process to master, but continued practice will help you develop a comfortable skill level.

Putting yourself in the shoes of a roving anthropologist, think back over your experiences in different cultural situations. Try to remember the specifics. Concentrate on the actions. Put aside for the moment your feelings about the situation and your feelings about how the other person was behaving. As you recall the incident, work through the following steps, which you can remember as "AHA" – assess, hypothesize, and act. Here's how it works.

**Assess.** As you recall the incident, try to remember what the people involved said and did. Write down or otherwise record your memory of what happened and how the people involved interacted. Describe the behaviors as you remember them. Don't speculate on the motives behind the behaviors.

**Hypothesize.** Review your descriptions. Why do you think this incident happened as it did? From what you have learned about cultural dimensions, think about how the dimensions might underlie some of the behaviors you described and record your responses. At the time of the incident, did you guess about what motivated the others involved? Did you guess about how people would act in that situation? How did you react to the behavior of others in the situation? Compare your review of the situation (with the benefit of your growing cultural awareness) with your memory of it – do you see the incident differently now? Were your guesses close or completely off target?

**Act.** Based on your best guess about the cultural dimensions that motivated the behaviors in this incident, how might you act in a similar situation now? Think about what you did at the time and what the response was from others. Did you predict that response at the time of the incident? What other actions might you have taken? What response do you think you would have gotten had you acted differently? When you begin to use this process in current situations, ask questions or take actions that will help you test your assumptions.

Using the AHA method for in-the-moment situations and for evaluating past interactions is a great way to learn from your experience and become more culturally adaptable. If you think you need more practice playing the part of a roving anthropologist, you can also use the AHA process in other situations. For example, just as you examined cultural dimensions and expectations by watching a foreign film, you can see the same film and use the AHA steps to analyze situations in which members of your native country interact with people of other countries and cultures. Granted, many of the interactions you see on the screen are simplistic and stereotypical, but they do give you a chance to think about what is happening culturally in the interaction, what you might do in similar circumstances, and what you might expect if you acted differently than the characters in the movie. As you did when reflecting on your own past situations, assess the situation depicted in the film by observing the actors and what they do. Hypothesize about what is happening based on your understanding of the different cultures presented in the film. Think about how you might act in particular scenes or how the characters might have acted differently to achieve different results.

You can also practice the AHA approach in daily conversations, even with people with whom you share some basic cultural aspects. A conversation with a colleague who is of a different race, gender, or age provides plenty of chances for you to assess, hypothesize, and act in ways that bolster your cultural intelligence.

# Cultural Adaptability at Work

The potential advantages of developing cultural adaptability as a leadership skill become more evident the longer you practice and the more often you find yourself working with others who are different from yourself. If you can make a fairly accurate guess about the kind of behavior that is likely to make a colleague react negatively because of cultural differences, that information can help you avoid or resolve a conflict. An ability to understand underlying cultural motivations and anticipate potential disagreements in a culturally significant situation will help you create more effective working relationships across cultural boundaries. It takes time to become proficient at this skill. Some managers spend decades living and working in other countries learning how to do this well. But once you are comfortable with the process you can continue to build your cultural awareness and develop your cultural adaptability. That ability gives you a real advantage in managing and leading in an increasingly diverse and complex world.

## Suggested Readings

Dalton, M., Ernst, C., Deal, J., & Leslie, J. (2002). *Success for the new global manager: How to work across distances, countries, and cultures.* San Francisco: Jossey-Bass.

Elashmawi, F. (2001). *Competing globally: Mastering multicultural management and negotiations.* Boston: Butterworth-Heinemann.

Hofstede, G. (2001). *Culture's consequences: Comparing values, behaviors, institutions, and organizations across nations* (2nd ed.). London: Sage.

Leslie, J. B., Dalton, M., Ernst, C., & Deal, J. (2002). *Managerial effectiveness in a global context.* Greensboro, NC: Center for Creative Leadership.

Prince, D. W., & Hoppe, M. H. (2000). *Communicating across cultures.* Greensboro, NC: Center for Creative Leadership.

Rhinesmith, S. (1996). *A manager's guide to globalization* (2nd ed.). Chicago: Irwin.

Rosen, R. (2000). *Global literacies: Lessons on business leadership and national cultures.* New York: Simon & Schuster.

Storti, C. (2001). *The art of crossing cultures.* Yarmouth, ME: Intercultural Press.

Trompenaars, F. (1993). *Riding the waves of culture: Understanding cultural diversity in business.* London: The Economist Books.

Walker, D. M., Walker, T., & Schmitz, J. (2003). *Doing business internationally: The guide to cross-cultural success.* New York: McGraw-Hill.

Wilson, M., Hoppe, M. H., & Sayles, L. R. (1996). *Managing across cultures: A learning framework.* Greensboro, NC: Center for Creative Leadership.

# Background

In 1998 CCL began a research project designed to answer questions about managerial effectiveness and how it applied to managers who work in an increasingly complex global work environment. What do they do? Is it different from the work they did when they managed in their own countries, and if so, how is it different? What does it take for these managers to be effective when they manage across so many countries simultaneously? What do they need to know to be effective?

One of the issues to arise from that study (documented in a technical report, *Managerial Effectiveness in a Global Context*, and further explored for practicing managers in the book *Success for the New Global Manager*) was the idea of *cultural adaptability*. CCL defined cultural adaptability as a person's ability to deal with the stress caused by cultural differences so that he or she can continue to learn.

To make this knowledge accessible to leaders participating in CCL's educational programs, the project's researchers developed a curriculum for teaching managers how they might develop their potential for cultural adaptability. Other subject matter experts at CCL, most notably Maxine Dalton, Michael Hoppe, and Meena Wilson, contributed an understanding of cultural dimensions to this effort. This guidebook couples that learning framework with research findings and firsthand experience drawn from CCL's own international faculty. It develops and disseminates that collective knowledge, and it reflects CCL's belief that interacting effectively with others who are different from oneself is a skill that can be learned through experience and over time.

# Key Point Summary

The workforce is much more diverse now than it was in the past, and it is anticipated to become even more so in the future. Stretching your ability to effectively interact with others who come from a different culture than yours calls for a new kind of flexibility for handling differences and change – cultural adaptability. It demands willingness and an ability to recognize and understand cultural differences, and to work effectively across them. Those differences affect expectations, approaches to work, views of authority, and other issues. By developing the skill of cultural adaptability, your interactions with people who are different from you have a better chance of producing successful outcomes.

Developing cultural adaptability requires that you examine your own cultural foundations, that you expect to encounter cultural differences, that you educate yourself about different cultures, and that you learn from your cross-cultural experiences. For managers who want to be or to remain successful in a global environment, cultural adaptability is a vital leadership skill.

# ORDERING INFORMATION

To order additional Ideas Into Action guidebooks, please contact us by phone at **336 545 2810** or visit our online bookstore at **www.ccl.org/publications**. Prepayment is required for all orders under $100.

Ongoing Feedback: How to Get It, How to Use It (#400) $9.95

Reaching Your Development Goals (#401) $9.95

Becoming a More Versatile Learner (#402) $9.95

Giving Feedback to Subordinates (#403) $9.95

Three Keys to Development: Defining and Meeting Your Leadership Challenges (#404) $9.95

Feedback That Works: How to Build and Deliver Your Message (#405) $9.95

Communicating Across Cultures (#406) $9.95

Learning from Life: Turning Life's Lessons into Leadership Experience (#407) $9.95

Keeping Your Career on Track: Twenty Success Strategies (#408) $9.95

Preparing for Development: Making the Most of Formal Leadership Programs (#409) $9.95

Choosing an Executive Coach (#410) $9.95

Setting Your Development Goals: Start with Your Values (#411) $9.95

Do You Really Need a Team? (#412) $9.95

Building Resiliency: How to Thrive in Times of Change (#413) $9.95

How to Form a Team: Five Keys to High Performance (#414) $9.95

Using Your Executive Coach (#415) $9.95

Managing Conflict with Your Boss (#416) $9.95

How to Launch a Team: Start Right for Success (#417) $9.95

Managing Conflict with Direct Reports (#418) $9.95

Managing Conflict with Peers (#419) $9.95

Maintaining Team Performance (#420) $9.95

Making Creativity Practical: Innovation That Gets Results (#421) $9.95

Developing Cultural Adaptability: How to Work Across Differences (#422) $9.95

Leading Dispersed Teams (#423) $9.95

Feedback Guidebook Package (#724; includes #400, #403, #405) $19.95

Development Guidebook Package (#726; includes #401, #404, #409, #411) $29.95

Conflict Guidebook Package (#731; includes #416, #418, #419) $19.95

Teams Guidebook Package (#732; includes #412, #414, #417, #420, #423) $39.95

U.S. shipping (UPS Ground – $4 for 1st book; $0.95 each additional book)
Non-U.S. shipping (Express International – $20 for 1st book; $5 each additional book)
CCL's Federal Tax ID #23-707-9591

Single title quantity discounts: 2-49 – $8.95; 50-99 – $7.95; 100-499 – $6.50; 500+ – $5.95